The Nature Kid's Guide to GRASSHOPPERS

Level 2

DAVID ANDERSON

LP Media Inc. Publishing
Text copyright © 2026 by LP Media Inc.
All rights reserved.

For information address LP Media Inc. Publishing,
30012 Variolite St NW, Princeton MN 55371
www.lpmedia.org

Publication Data

Grasshoppers
The Nature Kid's Guide to Grasshoppers — First edition.

Summary: "Learn all about Grasshoppers, the Nature Kid Way"
— Provided by publisher.

ISBN: 979-8-89818-218-2

[1. Grasshoppers – Non-Fiction] I. Title.

Title: The Nature Kid's Guide to Grasshoppers

CONTENTS

GRASSY GROUNDS

4

Zzzip! A red-legged grasshopper jumps across a sunny meadow.

Step outside on a warm sunny day and listen. That clicking, buzzing sound coming from the grass? That is a grasshopper, and this book is going to show you everything about them!

Grasshoppers live wherever plants grow thick and the sun shines warm. Fields, meadows, farms, and backyard gardens are all perfect homes. They need green leaves to eat and soft soil to bury their eggs safely underground.

Red-legged grasshoppers are one of the most common you will find. Peek into the grass on a warm afternoon and one might be looking right back at you!

GLOBAL HOPPERS

One locust swarm can have more grasshoppers in it than there are people on Earth — up to 80 billion!

Whoosh! A swarm of locusts flies over a wide desert.

Grasshoppers live on every continent except Antarctica. Hot deserts, cool mountains, thick forests — no matter the place, grasshoppers have found a way to make it work.

Some take things to an extreme. Migratory locusts swarm together by the billions across Africa and Asia. A single swarm can stretch for miles and blot out the sun like a living storm cloud!

Wherever you are in the world, grasshoppers are close by. From city parks to open farm fields, they have been hopping across this planet for over 250 million years.

TINY TITANS

The smallest grasshoppers are just half an inch long — they can sit on top of a dime!

Thud! A big lubber grasshopper lands on a fence post.

Most grasshoppers are about as long as your pinky finger — roughly one to two inches. They weigh less than a grape, but do not let that fool you. These tiny insects are incredibly strong for their size!

Some are much bigger though. The lubber grasshopper can grow up to three inches long, about as long as a crayon.

But even the biggest grasshopper is tiny next to you. Their secret is not size — it is what those little legs can do. You won't believe how far they can jump!

BODY BITS

A grasshopper has five eyes — two big compound eyes and three tiny simple eyes on top of its head!

10

Click! A Carolina grasshopper snaps its dark wings open.

A grasshopper has three main body parts. The head sits up front. The **thorax** is in the middle, where six legs attach. The **abdomen** is the long back part.

Most grasshoppers have two sets of wings. The front wings are tough like shields that protect the back wings. The back wings are thin and fold up like a fan when not in use.

Carolina grasshoppers have black back wings with a pale yellow band along the edge. You can spot this flash of color when they spread their wings to fly.

SUPER SENSES

Grasshoppers can feel tiny shakes in the ground through their feet — they sense footsteps before they see danger!

Whirr! A painted grasshopper hears danger and hides fast.

Grasshoppers have amazing senses. Their compound eyes can see in almost every direction at once. They can spot a hungry bird from far away, giving them plenty of time to escape.

Most animals hear with ears on their heads. Not grasshoppers! They hear with a round spot called a tympanum on each side of their belly.

They also have long **antennae** that help them smell food and sense the wind. Grasshoppers use all these senses together to stay safe in open fields.

HIDE WELL

A grasshopper's brown spit is called 'tobacco juice' — it can stain your fingers if you hold one!

Shh! A pallid-winged grasshopper sits still and blends into dry dirt.

Many grasshoppers hide in plain sight. Their colors match the dirt, grass, or leaves around them. This is called **camouflage**, and it keeps them safe from hungry eyes.

Pallid-winged grasshoppers are pale gray or tan. They look just like the sandy ground they sit on. A bird might fly right over without seeing them!

Some grasshoppers also spit out brown juice when scared. It tastes bad and makes predators want to leave them alone. Yuck!

LEAF LUNCH

A grasshopper can eat half its body weight in plants every single day — imagine eating 40 pounds of salad!

16

Crunch! A differential grasshopper chews through a fat green leaf.

Grasshoppers eat plants. They chew on grasses, leaves, flowers, and stems. Some will even munch on crops like wheat and corn.

Differential grasshoppers are big eaters. They can cause real trouble on farms by eating too many crops. Farmers watch out for them every summer.

A grasshopper chews with strong jaws that move side to side. They do not chew up and down like we do! Those sideways jaws can slice through tough stems with ease.

CHIRPY CHAT

Grasshoppers chirp faster when it is warm — you can almost guess the temperature by counting their chirps!

Chirp! A grasshopper rubs its legs and sings a tiny song.

Grasshoppers talk with sounds. They rub a bumpy back leg against a wing to make a chirpy noise. It is like running a stick along a comb!

Clear-winged grasshoppers also click when they fly. They snap their wings together in the air. Other grasshoppers nearby can hear these clicks from far away.

Each kind of grasshopper makes its own special sound. A chirp can mean 'stay away' or 'I am here.' Sound is how these bugs chat with each other!

HUNGRY HUNTERS

Praying mantises are one of the few insects that hunt grasshoppers!

Swoop! A bird dives down, but the painted grasshopper jumps just in time.

Many animals love to eat grasshoppers. Birds, frogs, lizards, and spiders all hunt them. Even mice and snakes will grab a grasshopper for a quick meal.

But the painted grasshopper has a clever trick. Its bright colors send a warning to predators — one bad taste and most animals never try again! Birds learn fast. After one painted grasshopper, they leave the colorful ones alone.

With so many hunters around, most grasshoppers must stay sharp. Good thing they are quick and full of clever tricks to stay safe!

JUMP AWAY

Some grasshoppers kick their predators with sharp spines on their back legs — ouch!

Boing! A grasshopper rockets into the air to dodge a bird.

Grasshoppers are built to jump. Their back legs work like loaded springs. One powerful push sends them flying through the air faster than you can blink. They can leap 20 times their own body length!

To pull off a jump like that, a grasshopper stores energy in a special pad near its knee. When it releases, the leg snaps straight in an instant. It is like a catapult built right into their body.

No running start needed. No warning. Just gone!

HIGH FLYERS

DID YOU KNOW?
If you could jump like a grasshopper, you could leap over a 10-story building in one bound!

Humm! A swarm of migratory locusts take to the sky.

When jumping is not enough, grasshoppers take to the air. Two pairs of wings fold flat against the body when resting, then snap open in flight. Those wings can carry them much farther than any jump.

Migratory locusts are the ultimate fliers. They travel over 80 miles in a single day, riding warm air currents high above the ground. Huge swarms fly together, covering entire continents over weeks.

Most grasshoppers fly to escape danger or find fresh food. Either way, those wings make them very hard to catch!

SUNNY DAYS

DID YOU KNOW?

On rainy days, grasshoppers hide under leaves and barely move — they need sunshine to stay active!

Sizzle! A grasshopper stretches out on a warm rock at sunrise.

Grasshoppers start their day by soaking up the sun. They need warmth to get their bodies moving. On cool mornings, they sit very still until the sun heats them up.

Once warm, they start to eat. Grasshoppers munch on plants all through the day. Many grasshoppers are most active during the hottest parts of the day.

When the sun goes down, grasshoppers slow down too. They find a leaf or stem to rest on and stay still all night. Then they wait for morning to start again.

SOLO LIFE

Locusts start out as loners. But when too many crowd together and keep bumping into each other, a chemical in their brain switches on and suddenly they join the swarm!

28

Rustle! A lone grasshopper perches on a stem all by itself.

Most grasshoppers live alone. They do not need a group to find food or stay safe. One grasshopper is perfectly happy all by itself.

But sometimes many show up in one place. This happens where food is easy to find. Young lubber grasshoppers often cluster together near their favorite plants.

Even in a crowd, grasshoppers do not work as a team. They just happen to be in the same spot at the same time. Each one looks out for itself.

LOVE SONGS

FUN
FACT!
A single female grasshopper can lay up to 300 eggs in her lifetime — that's a lot of baby hoppers!

Bzzz! A male grasshopper sings his heart out for a mate.

Male grasshoppers sing to get the attention of females. Each male makes his own special song. Females listen closely to pick the best singer.

The female hides in the grass and waits. If she likes what she hears, she moves closer. Red-legged grasshoppers sing loudest on warm, sunny days when the air carries sound well.

After mating, the female finds soft, damp soil. She digs a small hole with her abdomen and lays her eggs inside. Then she covers them up to keep them safe from harm.

TINY NYMPHS

DID YOU KNOW?
Grasshopper nymphs can hop just minutes after hatching — they are born ready to bounce!

Munch! A group of grasshopper nymphs just hatched and they are hungry!

Baby grasshoppers are called **nymphs**. They look like tiny adults but have no wings yet. A nymph is about the size of a grain of rice when it hatches!

Nymphs start eating right away. They munch on soft, young leaves. Differential grasshopper nymphs hatch in spring when plants are fresh and green.

As nymphs grow, they shed their skin five or six times. Each time, they get a little bigger. By summer, they look just like full-grown grasshoppers with wings.

GROW SOLO

DID YOU KNOW?

A grasshopper nymph grows from rice-sized baby to full adult in just about two months!

Pop! A female grasshopper lays her eggs in the soil. Then she leaves forever.

Grasshopper parents do not raise their young. Once the babies hatch, they are completely on their own. No one brings them food or keeps them warm.

Each nymph must find its own food and hiding spots. Clear-winged grasshopper nymphs wander off right after hatching. No one shows them where to go or what to eat.

This may seem tough, but it works. Grasshoppers have lived this way for millions of years. Each tiny nymph is born knowing exactly what to do.

BUILT TOUGH
DID YOU KNOW?
Most grasshoppers only live for about one year — but they pack a lot of hopping into that time!

Hiss! Hot desert wind blows, but the grasshopper hangs on.

Grasshoppers are tough little survivors. Their eggs stay safe underground all winter long. A foam covering protects them from cold, ice, and hungry beetles.

Pallid-winged grasshoppers live in dry deserts. They get most of their water from the plants they eat. Even in blazing heat, they find ways to stay cool by resting in shade.

Young grasshoppers can even regrow a lost leg! Each time a nymph molts and sheds its old skin, the new leg grows back a little more. After a few molts it is nearly full size again. Lose a leg, grow it back — not bad for a bug!

SPOT SOME

If you stand very still in a meadow, a curious grasshopper may land right on your shoe!

Swish! A grasshopper hops right past your feet in the grass.

Want to find grasshoppers? Head to a sunny field or park on any hot summer day. Walk slowly through the grass and watch for little jumps.

Carolina grasshoppers are easy to find. They often sit on dirt paths and sidewalks. When you get close, they fly up with a buzzing, clicking sound.

Be still and listen for tiny chirps. Watch one up close, then let it go. Every grasshopper helps keep nature healthy by feeding birds and spreading seeds. Treat them with care!

GLOSSARY

nymph

A young grasshopper that has not grown its wings yet

thorax

The middle section of an insect's body where legs attach

abdomen

The back section of an insect's body

antennae

Two thin feelers on an insect's head for smelling and touching

camouflage

Colors or patterns that help an animal blend in and hide